Brainstorming

Unleashing Your Creativity to Think Outside the Box

Sandra J. Hovatter

Published by

Data Designs Publishing

182 St. Mary's St.
Norwalk, OH 44857
419-660-0500
www.datadesignspublishing.com

Cover design by Matthew A. McMorrow

Brainstorming

Unleashing Your Creativity
to Think Outside the Box

Table of Contents

Chapter 1, Why Brainstorming?.. 3

Chapter 2, Preparing for Creativity 9

Chapter 3, Managing Creativity – Let the Fun Begin 21

Chapter 4, Preserving the Fruit of Your Creativity.......... 33

Chapter 5, Brainstorming, Party of One 39

Appendix 1 – Checklists 43

Appendix 2 – Brainstorming Guidelines.......................... 48

Chapter 1
Why Brainstorming?

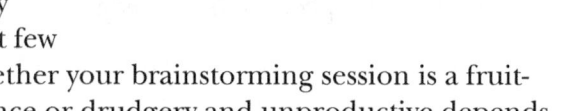

At one time or another, you have probably been a part of a brainstorming session. It's an activity everyone thinks they know how to do, but few people do well. Whether your brainstorming session is a fruitful and fun experience or drudgery and unproductive depends largely on how well it is planned and moderated.

Even just a little planning can increase the profitability of each brainstorming session you conduct...and a brainstorming session that isn't profitable is actually quite expensive. Poorly led brainstorming sessions lead to a lack of quality ideas. This leads either to implementing bad ideas or not making any changes. Both outcomes frustrate and demoralize who participated in the brainstorming sessions. Of course, that's exactly the opposite of what you were hoping to achieve.

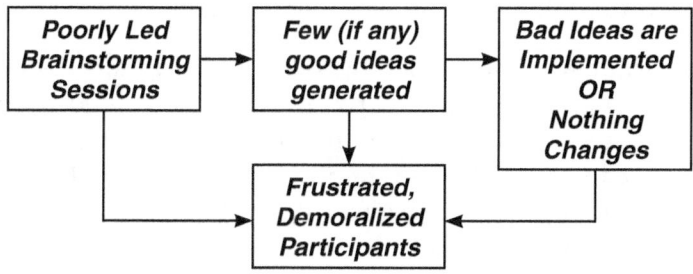

The cost of poorly planned and executed brainstorming sessions, then, includes the following:

- ➤ Cost of man hours to bring a group of people together
- ➤ Costs associated with implementing bad ideas generated at the brainstorming session

– OR –

- ➤ Costs associated with not implementing any solutions or better practices – that is, the cost of continuing "business as usual"
- ➤ Cost of having frustrated and demoralized participants/employees/members/customers
- ➤ Cost of loss of management credibility
- ➤ Cost of loss of future participation by those who have lost faith in the process and/or your management

You can avoid these costs by planning and implementing effective brainstorming sessions. This book provides instructions and ideas about how to conduct brainstorming sessions that bring out the most and the best ideas from all participants.

Overview

Brainstorming is an activity that can be done any time you need more ideas or fresher ideas to help move your project to the next level. That might mean new ideas for projects to pursue or innovative ideas for solving a problem. Brainstorming is appropriate not only in the business world, but can be used successfully in almost any situation. It can even be used to involve the whole family in planning your summer adventures.

Brainstorming was developed by Alex Osborn in the 1940s. Mr. Osborn was a founding partner in an advertising firm that was widely recognized as one of the most innovative agencies in New York City. He had an intense interest in stimulating creative thinking and wrote a number of books on the subject. He explained the process he used to foster creativity in his books *How to Think Up* and *Your Creative Power*. In the latter book, Osborn gave credit to the participants in the first group he organized to produce ideas:

> It was in 1939 when I first organized such a group in our company. The early participants dubbed our efforts **"Brainstorming Sessions"**; and quite aptly so because, in this case, "brainstorm" means using the **brain** to **storm** a creative problem – and do so in **commando** fashion, with each stormer attacking the same objective."

OK, that sounds just a little too militaristic to describe the brainstorming sessions of today, but the concept is the same – many people working together to generate fresh ideas. The brainstorming process stimulates creative thinking. It is a tremendously effective tool for generating new ideas or fresh spins on old ideas. (Note that recent studies refute this claim – see **Recent Research in Brainstorming** on the following page for more on this.)

Brainstorming is the process of allowing ideas to flow freely without any evaluation as to their value, reasonableness, cost effectiveness, achievability or anything else. This is critically important. When negative feedback is introduced into the brainstorming, it is perceived as criticism and people become more guarded in voicing the ideas that come to mind. Frequently, it is the most outrageous idea that sparks *the* idea that is eventually pursued.

Based on the process described above, you can surmise that there are two cardinal rules of brainstorming:

➢ There is no such thing as a bad idea.
➢ No criticism or negative feedback is allowed during the brainstorming session.

Have you ever watched ice crack? It begins slowly with a single crack, then builds speed as cracks appear around the original one. Some are big and some are small, but as each crack occurs, it causes more and more cracks to appear. Eventually the frequency of the cracking slows down. If you put just a little pressure on the ice, the process will start again.

Brainstorming is like ice cracking. As each idea is suggested, many other ideas branch from it. Some ideas come to you fully formed – big ideas that drop into your mind. Other ideas start

as a smaller fissure, slowly working their way to the surface of your mind. But once they reach the forefront and you express them, others follow closely behind. Eventually, new ideas come more slowly or stop altogether. Sometimes, a little pressure from an outside stimulant can start the process all over again.

This book will help you get the ice cracking and give you techniques for applying a little pressure when the ideas begin to come more slowly. Before we get into the depths of brainstorming, however, let's look at recent research which suggests that brainstorming is actually an anti-creativity exercise.

Recent Research in Brainstorming

Since the first empirical study of brainstorming in 1958, many studies have shown that brainstorming in groups yields fewer ideas than having the same number of people brainstorming on their own. Additionally, more of the ideas generated were possible to implement. It seems that working individually, each participant thought through the problem more thoroughly.

Additional studies have shown that altering one of Osborn's cardinal rule of brainstorming – that is, no criticism of ideas – fostered more creative thinking and practical ideas. One study even found that introducing wrong ideas – that is, ideas that were totally unworkable or didn't address the problem – and then allowing evaluation or discussion of those ideas fostered more creative thinking on the part of the participants.

My experience is that brainstorming is an effective tool for generating creative ideas in a group setting, but that Osborn's model can be modified a bit to get the best results. While it is true that studies have shown that more ideas are generated by individuals working alone to solve a problem, the studies have typically compared the results of a group of people generating ideas together to a group of the same number of people each generating ideas individually under the same conditions as the group – that is, not distracted by other things and for the same amount of time. The problem with this study is that disciplined individual brainstorming as required in the research doesn't happen in today's world of "always another deadline to meet, phone call to answer or task to make progress on."

> *One of the values of bringing a group together is controlling the environment and having a number of people focusing only on the subject at hand.*

Additionally, it isn't typical for a manager to assign the same problem to multiple people and have them return with as many ideas as possible.

> *A second value of bringing a group together is that more people are involved in finding a solution or generating the next great idea.*

Knowing the results of recent research allows us to modify our brainstorming approach and guidelines to get the most benefit from the activity.

Finally, an added benefit of brainstorming is that it can be quite effective in developing and encouraging a team to work together. A well planned, well implemented brainstorming session can increase the team's interdynamics as well as each participants' sense of ownership of the solution or idea implemented.

Chapter 2
Preparing for Creativity

Identifying Your Participants and Moderator

While spur of the moment brainstorming sessions can be productive, you'll find that putting a little effort into planning will yield a greater variety of ideas being generated by the group. Before discussing how to prepare for the brainstorming session, let's look at how to identify participants and select a moderator.

Going it Alone or Finding a Group

As discussed earlier, brainstorming research has shown that more ideas can be generated by individuals working alone instead of as part of a group. Even so, I much prefer group brainstorming because of the chain reaction of ideas that develop. Group brainstorming brings the varied experiences of a number of people together to focus on a problem or topic.

Not everyone has a group, however. We'll cover brainstorming with a group first. You'll find ideas to help you brainstorm alone in Chapter 4.

Identifying Your Brainstorming Group

Identifying your brainstorming group involves deciding how many people to include and who those people should be. We'll address both issues here and Appendix 1 provides a checklist to use when identifying your brainstorming group. You can find it on page 44.

Keep the group small. You'll want to gather a group of three to six individuals. If you have more than six people, you might consider breaking into two smaller groups. Each group can brainstorm the same topic or different aspects of the topic. Brainstorming with a group of more than six people is often counter-productive. One of two things is likely to happen:

> ➤ The group becomes unwieldy and the atmosphere quickly deteriorates into a party at which nothing of value is accomplished. Reigning in the partying brainstormers squashes the desire to bring ideas to the table.

> ➤ A few people continue to generate ideas, but those who may not think as quickly as others disengage and begin to check their emails, send text messages or count ceiling tiles. Trying to draw these individuals into the conversation when others are jumping forward with more and more ideas begins to feel like punishment, which again, doesn't promote new ideas.

Keep your group relatively small and you'll find that the interaction among participants is livelier and healthier.

Various backgrounds bring different experiences. It's important to gather a group of people with different backgrounds, perspectives and personalities. Five people with five different backgrounds and experiences are going to generate more ideas and a greater variety of ideas than people with similar backgrounds and experiences. When Joe, for example, who has spent the last ten years managing a non-profit organization, hears the idea of Alice, who has spent the last two years as a sales rep for a high tech company, he might first think it's crazy. After turning the idea around in his mind a bit, though, he's likely to offer a similar idea from a very different perspective. Jerry, who is a buyer for a small tools company, will hear both of their ideas and have a third take on them. And so on, and so on, and so on. You get the idea.

Different personality types yield more ideas. Likewise, people with different personalities approach situations and process information in different ways. For example, administrators tend to think in terms of goal setting. Goal setting may be meaningless to an engineer who thinks in terms of problem solving. Artistic types think visually, while scientists think conceptually. Bringing different types of people together for a brainstorming session can result in ideas that truly are out-side the box.

How well participants know one another impacts your success. In addition to selecting people of different backgrounds and personalities, getting the right mix of participants can impact your results. One study found that the worst results occurred in brainstorming sessions when:

> ➢ all the participants knew one another too well; or
> ➢ all participants didn't know one another well enough.

When all participants had worked together for quite awhile, the result was a lack of fresh ideas. When participants didn't know one another well enough, they were too uncomfort-able to take the risk of suggesting off-the-wall ideas. The best group is made up primarily of people who know one another well enough to risk suggesting unusual ideas with one or two people who are new to the group and therefore offer fresh perspectives.

Obviously your participants need to have enough in common to make them a reasonable choice to offer ideas on the issue being brainstormed – they might all have a common interest in the subject or all work for the same company or belong to the same organization. That's your starting point.

Take that starting point and build your team by adding diversity in backgrounds and personality types, then shake the group up a bit by adding someone the participants don't know as well. That should give you a great group for interact-ing well and coming up with unique and creative ideas.

If you regularly plan brainstorming sessions, be sure not to invite the same people to each session, regardless of whether the topics are similar or different. Vary the group to get the best results.

If your group ends up being people who do not know one another or don't work together often, you should consider doing a warm-up brainstorming session at the beginning of your meeting. See *Preparing the Presentation* on page 13 for more on this.

Selecting a Moderator

The brainstorming moderator plays a key role. He or she must prepare for the session, present the topic to the group, moderate as ideas begin to flow, and then bring closure to the process as the session ends. The moderator's responsibilities are explained in more detail throughout this chapter. Understanding these responsibilities are important when selecting the moderator.

Preparing for the Brainstorming Session

After the moderator has been selected, the real preparation for the brainstorming session begins. It is his or her responsibility to complete the following tasks:

- ➢ Decide on a brainstorming approach or technique
- ➢ Prepare the presentation
- ➢ Prepare the venue
- ➢ Gather supplies
- ➢ Invite group members
- ➢ Select a recorder
- ➢ Prepare for what comes after the brainstorming session

Obviously the moderator will need to spend a bit of time preparing for the session. Each of these tasks is discussed in more detail in the following paragraphs.

The *Moderator Responsibilities Checklist* on page 45 is provided to help track your preparation.

Deciding on an Approach or Technique

Will your brainstorming use the standard, tried and true approach, or will you use a modified approach? Read Chapter 3 to learn the basic approach to brainstorming as well as several alternate techniques. These options to the basic approach can add a bit of spice to your session and work well for groups that are extraordinarily shy or groups that brainstorm together often.

Preparing the Presentation

Presenting the topic to the group in ways that unlock the maximum creative potential of each member is critical. The moderator should consider the members of the brainstorming group as he or she prepares this initial presentation. Are the group members conceptual or concrete thinkers? Are they goal or process oriented? The purpose is to present the topic so that group members fully grasp it while encouraging them to use their experience, knowledge, opinions, and interaction with one another to unleash their creativity.

It is also during this time that the moderator will set the group at ease. If the participants are a group of people who have never worked together before, the moderator should consider a practice or warm-up brainstorming session during the first few minutes. During this practice session, the group can brainstorm about a somewhat ridiculous topic. It will break the ice and get people comfortable with the process.

An effective presentation will do the following:

> ➤ Include two or three elements:
>> ➤ Presentation of the problem, issue, or topic being brainstormed.
>> ➤ Presentation of guidelines for good brainstorming. (See Appendix 1 for guidelines that you may copy and provide to participants.)

> Practice or warm-up session if appropriate.

> Be brief. Don't bore your brainstorming team then ask them to be creative. Be succinct in your presentation of both the topic and the brainstorming guidelines.

  When all is said and done, you ought to be able to present the topic for brainstorming in one or two sentences.

> Define the problem, issue, or topic being brainstormed properly. Think through the purpose of the brainstorming session carefully before defining the topic. You don't want to waste time and money brainstorming the wrong problem.

> Restate the topic, perhaps in a slightly different way. You want to make sure everyone is on the same page before you get started.

> Allow time for questions to be sure everyone understands the topic being brainstormed.

> Ensure that the group is comfortable with the process and one another. The moderator should create a warm-up question for the group to practice with if the participants aren't comfortable with one another. Here are some ideas:

  > You are at a small dinner gathering at a friend's house and find a cockroach in your salad. How can you handle this?

  > Let's brainstorm chapter titles for a book I'm writing about brainstorming.

  > How can we change the world without spending more than $50?

  > What could your local sports team do to generate more ticket sales?

As part of the process of preparing the presentation, the moderator should develop several questions and ideas to help foster the generation of ideas:

> Develop several questions that you might use to start the brainstorming session after you present the topic. The

questions should address the topic, but be asked a different way or from a different perspective to stimulate the thinking of different group members.

➢ Develop five or six questions that you can use to foster creativity during the brainstorming session. Don't dump all of the questions on the group at once, but sprinkle them in over time to reinvigorate the group's discussion. The questions might suggesting a different perspective to view the topic from or a different challenge inherent in the topic.

For example, let's say that the family is gathered to brainstorm summer outings. The moderator would first explain the parameters for the outings (such as how much time and money are available), then be ready with some questions like these:

➢ What kinds of activities or trips would be fun and adventurous for you?

➢ Hot or cold? Wet or dry? Rustic or luxurious? What activities meet these criteria?

➢ Quickly! Name things you've been wanting to do within an hour's drive of home.

➢ Develop a couple of outrageous ideas that you can throw into the discussion when creativity wanes.

➢ Let's take grandma parasailing! (OK, in some families, that might be a normal activity, but in mine it would be pretty outrageous!)

Preparing the Venue

Where you conduct your brainstorming meeting can have a significant impact on it's success. We recommend holding your brainstorming session outside your normal environment. It is surprising how much this impacts the creative flow of ideas. If you're holding your brainstorming session in the same conference room that weekly staff meetings are held, people walk in with a "staff meeting" mindset. What usually happens at staff meetings? People report on their progress and receive new assignments. That mindset isn't conducive to free-flow brainstorming. Instead, find a comfortable location, then make it as inviting as possible. See ***Making Your Brainstorming Sessions More Fun and Productive*** on page 39 for more ideas.

Inviting Group Members

I have already discussed how to select group members for your brainstorming session. Once you have identified group members and selected a venue, invite each person. Be sure to require an RSVP so that you can ask additional people if some members are not able to attend.

Gathering Supplies

All ideas should be recorded in a way that is visible to everyone, so use either a smart board, chalkboard, poster board size paper, a computer projected on a screen/wall, or something similar. When participants can see the ideas that are generated, it helps them focus and generate more ideas.

If you've decided to use one of the alternate brainstorming techniques described in Chapter 3, you'll need to gather the supplies needed for that method.

Lastly, gather supplies you need to make the brainstorming session more fun and productive. See ***Making Your Brainstorming Sessions More Fun and Productive*** (page 39) for specific ideas.

Selecting a Recorder

The moderator will also want to select a recorder to post the ideas for the group as they are being generated. A good recorder can really help stimulate the group, while a poor one easily brings the flow of creativity to a standstill. The recorder must be able to encapsulate ideas into a few short words and write them quickly for the group to see. If the process takes too long for each idea, the group is spending more time watching the recorder than allowing their ideas to bounce off one another. If the description that is written doesn't capture the idea well, it affects all ideas that follow it and adds confusion when ideas are evaluated after the session.

Preparing for Post-Brainstorming

What happens when the brainstorming session ends? That's an important question to answer before you even start the session. Will the group do any evaluation of the ideas at the end of the session? Will you be bringing the group back together to refine any of the ideas? Will you or another group make decisions about which ideas to pursue? How will you communicate the outcome of the session to participants?

It's important to make these decisions before you begin your brainstorming session and communicate them to your group. In fact, your initial presentation to the brainstorming group should include a description of what happens next. Don't leave the group wondering if their effort has been a waste of their time.

Having a clear plan for what happens after the brainstorming session helps you to end the session effectively and communicate appropriately with your team members.

Moderating the Brainstorming Session

During the brainstorming session, the moderator has the following responsibilities:

- ➢ Present the topic to the group
- ➢ Moderate the flow of ideas
- ➢ Close the session well
- ➢ Follow-up with participants
- ➢ Initiate the idea evaluation process if appropriate

Presenting the Topic

Be upbeat while presenting the topic to your brainstorming group. Don't let questions take you off topic in your presentation. Answer those that address the group's understanding of the topic; defer others for a later discussion.

Explain your role as moderator – that is, it's your responsibility to bring the group back to the topic when they stray and to remind participants of the process if it begins to break down.

Moderate the brainstorming session

Once brainstorming has begun, the moderator's primary role is to enforce the "no criticism of ideas" rule and to strike the balance between letting outrageous ideas flow while still keeping the group on topic. Without the moderator continually bringing participants back to the topic at hand, the group is likely to get off track as they follow the path of one of the more outrageous ideas.

See Chapter 3 for more guidelines on how to moderate the session and for alternate brainstorming techniques.

Initiate the Idea Evaluation Process if Appropriate

Evaluating the ideas generated may begin at the end of the brainstorming session or after the session has ended. Have a plan for evaluating the ideas before you begin the brainstorming session. If it calls for the evaluation to begin with the entire group, do so when you have an appropriate amount of time remaining. See *After Your Brainstorming Session* on page 33 for more about how you might approach the evaluation process.

Close the Session Well and Follow-up with Participants

Some people think quickly on their feet and will generate many ideas during the brainstorming session. Others process information more slowly and reflectively. They might need a day or two to absorb all that has been thrown at them. Be sure to let everyone know that they can submit new ideas after the brainstorming session is concluded. Set a date when those ideas would no longer be useful.

Thank the participants and tell them what to expect next. See *After Your Brainstorming Session* (page 33) for more about what happens after your brainstorming session is finished.

After your brainstorming session is finished, be sure to provide feedback to your participants in the way you told them to expect.

Making Your Brainstorming Sessions More Fun and Productive

A fun brainstorming session is typically more productive than a boring one. There should be absolutely no pressure on the group to develop a specific number of ideas or achieve a specific purpose other than generate ideas. Pressure inhibits creative thinking in most people. As you plan your brainstorming session, consider how you might make it more fun. Here are some ideas:

➢ Sights, sounds, colors and smells can trigger different areas of the brain and thought processes. Use these things to trigger creativity.

   ➢ If you are brainstorming about an existing product or idea, having a tangible representation of the product or idea will help keep people focused.

   ➢ If you are brainstorming about a design, surround the staff with shapes and colors.

   ➢ If you are brainstorming about a process, background music that mirrors the type of process might be appropriate – that is, high-tempo music for a rapid process or quite jazz for a calm process (such as better customer service in a doctor's office).

   ➢ Brainstorming the marketing of a product targeted at men? How about incorporating a faint scent of a campfire into your planning?

➢ Hold your brainstorming session outside your normal environment. It is surprising how much this impacts the creative flow of ideas. If you're meeting in the same conference room that weekly staff meetings are held, people walk in with a "staff meeting" mindset. If, however, you can hold the meeting over breakfast rolls at a nearby coffee shop, people come ready to relax instead of ready to tense up. (I don't mean to imply that your staff meetings create tension but they probably are the vehicle for asking about progress and handing out assignments.)

Holding brainstorming sessions off-site provides the

added bonus of removing distractions from coworkers or bosses who have just a "quick question" to ask. Those quick questions will kill the momentum of your brainstorming session.

➢ Use props to help jump-start the creative process. If you are brainstorming about something with a theme, bring the theme into the session either through food, drink, environment, dress, posters, prizes, etc.

For example, if you're brainstorming about how to improve customer service, have some photos representative of your customers and ask the group what their needs and challenges are. Again, be careful not to overdo the theme or it becomes a distraction from the brainstorming activity.

➢ Provide a little food and drink – it can make the time together more relaxing. Be careful not to overdo it, though, or the food and drink will become a distraction to the brainstorming activity.

➢ Have a couple of seriously outside-the-box ideas to shout out to get the session started or when ideas are slow in coming.

➢ Offer a prize for what seems at first glance to be the most creative idea. (Remember, we're not evaluating the ideas at this time, so in the end that creative idea may never be used. You're rewarding creative thinking.) You might offer several of these prizes throughout the session when someone makes a great or ridiculous idea. Or simply say something like "Give that woman another muffin – Sara, that was a great idea!" Don't turn the session into a circus but have fun with it.

Remember that you want to keep your group on track, so only use sights, sounds, props, and unusual locations when then will help your group generate better ideas. Don't use them for the sake of using them. Creativity in this area is a good thing, but restraint is also a good thing.

Chapter 3
Managing Creativity –
Let the Fun Begin

Brainstorming Made Simple

So how does brainstorming actually work? Brainstorming is one of the easiest activities to organize and moderate. While there are sophisticated brainstorming techniques, I've always found that simpler approaches help people focus on the brainstorming topic instead of on the rules or process of the brainstorming session. The following paragraphs describe a simple approach to brainstorming. You'll find additional techniques later in this chapter.

The Standard Process

Once your moderator has properly prepared and you've gathered your group together, you're ready to begin brainstorming.

The process is described below. Appendix 1 provides the ***Brainstorming Process At-A-Glance Checklist***. Use this checklist as a reference during the brainstorming session. Also, you might modify the process below by incorporating one of the brainstorming techniques described later in this chapter.

> ➢ Present the brainstorming topic to the group. (See ***Preparing for the Brainstorming Session*** on page 12 for information about how to prepare the presentation and how to present it to the group.)

- ➢ Explain to the group how the brainstorming session will be run; that is, using the approach described in this chapter. Appendix 1 provides **Brainstorming Guidelines** beginning page 48. You may copy these guidelines and provide them to participants.
- ➢ Encourage participants to shout out any and all ideas.
- ➢ Remind participants that there is no such thing as a bad (or wrong) idea in brainstorming.
- ➢ Encourage participants to shout out ideas that are not even fully formed. Often these half-thoughts become fully formed as the whole group hears the seed of an idea.
- ➢ The recorder should add every idea to the list. Sometimes using different colors or shapes can spark more creativity. Always have several different colored markers for this purpose.

  Be sure to have plenty of wall space on which to record ideas.
- ➢ Do not allow any criticism of the ideas. When someone says "but that would…" say something like "let's set that aside right now – we'll evaluate how to implement ideas later." This is a cardinal rule of brainstorming as it was originally created.
  - ➢ Recent research has shown, however, that allowing some evaluation or discussion can yield better ideas. If the moderator thinks there is value in pursuing the objection, he or she might say something like "that's true, but let's jump off the idea with another idea that solves that problem (or that addresses that issue)." Just be careful not to get bogged down in digging too deeply on one idea before you've generated as many unique ideas as you'd like to see from the group.
  - ➢ When allowing evaluation and/or discussion of ideas, be sure that the conversation doesn't turn too negative as this will inhibit the free flow of ideas during the remainder of the session.

- Do not allow discussion of the ideas, except for what is required to understand it. As described above, you might allow some further discussion, but limit it based on the approach you want to take in brainstorming.

- Encourage those who generate ideas, no matter how insignificant or off the wall they may be.

- Encourage the participants not to be constrained by current processes, conventional wisdom about the topic, practicality, budgets or their boss's favorite approach.

- Allow time for thinking, but keep the session moving fairly quickly. At first, answers may come a little slowly. The group should relax within a short period of time and ideas will flow more freely.

- When you reach the point where ideas have slowed down, crack the ice by seeding the discussion with questions you prepared for just that purpose. They may encourage the participants to look at the topic from a different angle or look more closely at a specific element within the topic. Be careful not to take your brainstorming topic too far afield.

- Set a flexible time limit. Typically, thirty to sixty minutes is a good guideline. If you are including a time for evaluation at the end of your brainstorming session, you might extend the total duration to seventy-five or eighty minutes. Remember, brainstorming is hard work; don't schedule or continue the session for too long.

- Generally, end the brainstorming session when you've reached your time limit or exhausted your ideas, whichever comes first. If you've reached your time limit but ideas are still flowing freely, consider extending the session, but be aware that people tend to tire quickly after about forty-five minutes of active brainstorming.

- If appropriate, spend an additional ten to twenty minutes organizing your list of ideas. Sometimes this is better done with the whole group, sometimes by a smaller group or by a single person. Organizing your ideas is discussed in Chapter 4.

> ➤ Remember to end your brainstorming session by telling the group how the ideas they have generated will be evaluated and what future communication they can expect about the results of the brainstorming session.

Brainstorming Techniques – Going Beyond the Basics

While the basic approach to brainstorming described above can be quite productive, if you conduct regular brainstorming sessions you'll want to add some variety. Using alternate techniques can also help generate more ideas when brainstorming some types of topics or with some types of groups.

Alphabet Soup Style Brainstorming

I use this method more as therapy than as a brainstorming technique – any time I need to strongly distract myself from something that is going on around me (like an unpleasant medical test). But it lends itself to brainstorming.

Begin by preparing sheets for the recorder with every letter of the alphabet. It is the goal of the brainstorming participants to develop an idea that starts with each letter of the alphabet. Remember not to put pressure on the participants. Use some of the more difficult letters (Q or X perhaps) to add fun to the session, not pressure.

You can approach this technique several different ways:
1) Have participants shout out ideas as in standard brainstorming while the recorder writes the ideas next to the appropriate letter of the alphabet.
2) Have participants shout out ideas in alphabetical order – that is, ask for ideas for the letter A, then B, etc. until you've reached Z.
3) Work your way around the circle of participants asking them to provide an idea for each letter of the alphabet.

4) Instead of working your way around the circle, after each person gives an idea, they can challenge anyone else in the group to provide an idea for the next letter of the alphabet.

Be sure to keep the atmosphere positive and no-pressure.

Card Shuffle Brainstorming

This method is quite different in that the room will be much more quiet than in typical brainstorming. After the moderator has presented the topic, hand out 3" x 5" cards to each person. Have each person record two or three ideas on different cards. This process should take only a couple of minutes. Then have everyone pass their cards to the right.

Each person then takes the cards they received, select one, read the idea and then write any ideas they get based on the idea on the card. If they finish writing their ideas based on that card, they can go to the next card and go through the same process. This round should take three to five minutes. The moderator should judge when to move from round to round.

Repeat the process by having everyone pass the cards they are now holding to the right. Each person is now holding cards that have been written on by one or two people. They will do the same as in the previous round.

Repeat the process no more than five rounds, but stop sooner if it seems that the participants are laboring to develop ideas.

After card shuffling has stopped, the moderator can go into a more standard brainstorming session with participants sharing ideas from the cards they are currently holding.

Circles – We Got Circles

This method works well for individual brainstorming, but can also be used for a group. After presenting the topic to be brainstormed, the recorder should draw circles of various sizes and in various locations in the ideas area. Don't make the circles the same size and don't put them in straight line. They should be random. Using multiple colors is helpful. Then ask people for ideas to fill the circles. Record big ideas in big circles. For ideas that aren't fully formed, the recorder might add the idea than draw a cloud around it.

Remember not to evaluate ideas. An idea in a big circle isn't better than an idea in a small circle. It's simply a visual way to get ideas flowing.

From Here to There Brainstorming

This method is good for finding solutions to a problem – situations in which you can identify where you are now and where you want to be. During the moderator's presentation he or she will identify a starting place (here – i.e., where you are now) and an ending place (there – where you want to be). The team's goal is to identify solutions that will take you from here to there.

Begin by defining where you are on a sheet of paper or sticky note. Place it at the beginning or left side of the idea area. Write the solution on another sheet of paper or sticky note. Place it at the end or right side of the idea area. Then ask the group to fill in the blank.

As ideas are generated, they should be added to the idea area. Some ideas may be global or comprehensive – that is, they move from here to there by themselves. Others are steps in the journey from here to there. Place these of ideas closest to "here" or "there," depending where the step would fall in the process. In other words, if it is a first step, place the idea near "here;" if it is one of the final steps, place it near "there."

Remember, you're not committing to any of the ideas as you place them on the Here to There board. They are brainstorming ideas just as in standard brainstorming. Evaluation will occur after the brainstorming has been completed.

"If I Were King" Brainstorming

This method approaches brainstorming from the perspective of allowing each participant to assume they had ultimate authority to solve the problem being brainstormed. After presenting the topic, the moderator asks the question "If you were king, how would you solve this?" You can foster more ideas or approaching the problem from a different perspective by asking similar questions. After receiving several answers to the question, you can encouraging brainstorming based on one or more of the answers.

Here are some sample questions:

> "If you were king, what part of the current process would you keep?"
> "If you were king, what part of the current process would you absolutely delete or drop?"
> "If you were king, what piece of the problem would you attack first?"
> "If you were king, how would you rephrase the topic or problem?"

Opposites Attract Brainstorming

This method works well when thrown into a standard brainstorming session as new ideas are beginning to wane. The concept is to view the topic, problem or issue from the opposite direction or side. If for example, the problem was how to get more website traffic, you might say "Imagine that we had too much website traffic – what did we do to get it?"

Just Say It! Brainstorming

In this method, the moderator (or other participants) prompt participants to "Just say it!" After presenting the topic to be brainstorming and starting a standard brainstorming session, the moderator senses that some participants are holding back because of shyness, fear of being wrong or not having a fully developed idea in their minds. The moderator looks at the participant and says "Just say it!" encouraging the participant to say whatever is in their mind. Once the group catches on, they catch the look in other participants' eyes when they are on the cusp of an idea but reluctant to share and challenge one another to "Just say it!"

Mind Mapping

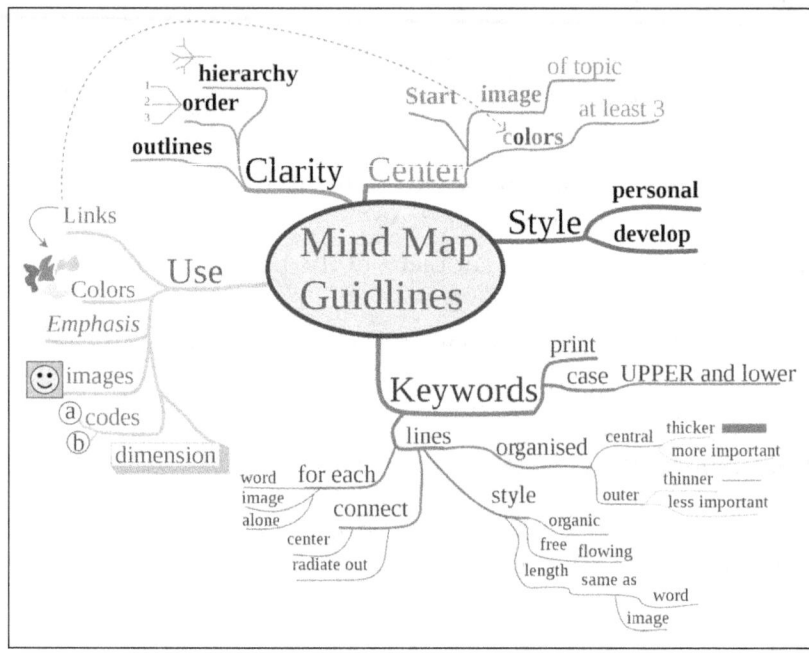

Mind Map of the Mind Map Guidelines
©User:Nicoguaro / Wikimedia Commons / CC-BY-SA-3.0

Mind mapping is the process of diagramming a series of related thoughts, and is illustrated in the above mind map. (Note that the above mind map is quite orderly. Those created freehand are often not nearly as "pretty.") Mind mapping lends itself to brainstorming because it visually portrays the haphazard process and result of brainstorming.

It is a blend of the logical and the creative, making it ideal for brainstorming and especially helpful in brainstorming alone. Typically, a mind map has a center idea from which all other ideas branch. Additional thoughts and ideas may branch off the main thought or any one of the branches. Colors are often introduced to relate ideas thematically.

As each idea is generated, add it to the mind map by drawing a line from the idea that was the inspiration for the new idea. Your mind map might look something like this.

While he certainly didn't invent the idea of "mind mapping," British psychologist and author Tony Buzan is credited with popularizing it in the early 1970s. When introduced to mind maps, my reaction was that they were simply outlines that radiated from a center instead of from the top down. That's basically the concept, but Buzan would argue that an outline forces readers to assimilate the material as one reads – from left to right and top to bottom. Buzan and other brain researchers have found that we actually scan entire pages in a non-linear fashion.

Personally, I tend to be the linear, left to right, top to bottom reader. Nevertheless, I've found mind mapping to be effective when organizing topics that were straining my outlines. Similarly, they can be effective brainstorming tools.

There are a number of software programs that can help with mind mapping. Here are two simple and inexpensive (or free) software applications for mindmapping:

http://www.mindapp.com/ – This is the software I use. It's inexpensive and easy to use.

http://www.mindmeister.com/ – A free software that is simple and highly rated.

Others are available. Google "mind mapping software" or "mind mapping software reviews" for more information.

Speed Round Brainstorming

This method can be intimidating to some participants. It is best suited for people who are high energy, quick thinkers, and not easily intimidated.

The goal of speed round brainstorming is to identify a specific number of ideas within a certain period of time.

The moderator identifies during his or her presentation the number of ideas and/or period of time for the speed round sessions. After the moderator completes the presentation, the timer starts and participants shout ideas as quickly as possible.

Having a second recorder can be helpful in speed round brainstorming to make sure you captured all of the ideas being generated

A variant of this approach is to give participants a short period of time to speed round brainstorm on their own, writing their own ideas, then begin standard brainstorming. Participants can share the ideas from their individual speed round brainstorming throughout the standard brainstorming session.

Similarly, you could break the entire group into two or three smaller groups, conduct a speed round of brainstorming, then bring the group together for a more standard brainstorming session.

Split Personality Brainstorming

This method challenges people to think about the topic from different perspectives. During the preparation phase, the moderator will identify various roles of people involved in the problem being brainstormed. Let's say you're brainstorming how to improve a product, for example. Those involved might be customers, bosses, factory workers, suppliers, salesmen, marketing, etc. Note that identifying these roles could be the first step in your brainstorming process with your group.

You could then proceed with brainstorming normally, reinforcing that each person should think about the topic from their assigned perspective. If you take this approach, you might want to designate an area of the idea board for each role rather than record all ideas in the same list.

Another approach with this method is to have your brainstormers break into groups based on their roles for a period of time. Be sure each group identifies a recorder to document their ideas. Then bring the group together and list all ideas and have a joint brainstorming session in which participants can abandon their roles and make suggestions from any perspective.

"What If" Brainstorming

This method changes the reality of the problem by asking the question "What if..." Finish the question by removing one of the parameters of the problem or one of the brainstorming ideas. For example, if we are brainstorming the packaging design for a new product, you might ask "What if using cardboard was not an option?" or "What if the product required safe handling?" If one of the most popular ideas was to package the product in formed foam rubber, you might ask "What if that was too expensive – what other ideas do you have?" Or conversely "What if we wanted to step it up a notch – make it nicer – what similar ideas do you have?"

Chapter 4
Preserving the Fruit of Your Creativity

After Your Brainstorming Session

When you have finished with the group brainstorming, it's time to begin to look at the ideas more objectively. Obviously, there was a purpose in identifying as many new and fresh ideas as possible. The next task is to review the ideas and identify which ideas to pursue or investigate further. Reviewing the ideas involves a process of categorizing, combining, expanding or condensing, and refining the ideas. This will then lead to a selection of which ideas to further evaluate and/or implement.

Before you begin your brainstorming session, decide whether you want the entire group to help with this process, a subset of the brainstorming group or a specific person from the group (often the moderator). If the entire group will be involved, be sure to keep the evaluation session short or schedule an additional meeting for this purpose.

Remember to communicate the results of the brainstorming session and the subsequent evaluation and implementation of the ideas with those who participated in your brainstorming session.

Follow these guidelines to evaluate the ideas generated during your brainstorming session:

Pre-Evaluation

➤ Immediately after the brainstorming session, review your notes to ensure that they are specific and sufficient enough for you to remember what the ideas were when you come back to them after setting them aside for a day or more. Spend about half an hour enhancing your notes as necessary.

➤ Set all your notes aside at least overnight. Depending on your personality, the brainstorming session itself may be draining or invigorating. You don't want to approach the evaluation process in either condition.

    ➤ If you're already drained of energy, you're most likely to select ideas that require the least amount of effort, not the best ideas.

    ➤ If you're invigorated, you may select ideas that are too overreaching or which appeal to you emotionally but have no practicality.

Organize Your List

➤ After setting your notes aside for a day or so, review the list briefly to combine items on the list that are simply different ways of saying the same thing or ideas that are so closely aligned that you wouldn't do one without the other. If the list generated from your brainstorming session isn't too scribbled and "ugly" you may be able to accomplish this task by circling like items, drawing arrows, etc. Most likely you'll find yourself rewriting (or retyping) the list during this process. (There's nothing wrong with ugly lists – they are often the sign of a very productive brainstorming session.)

➤ The next task is to organize the list in a way that makes sense for your project. This involves a little evaluation, but not extensive evaluation of the ideas.

For example, when we publish books for clients, we include a marketing brainstorming session with them.

The purpose of the brainstorming session is to generate ideas from which we develop a unique marketing plan. After one of these sessions, we organize the long list of ideas as follows:

General Ideas – Ideas that could be combined with any of the other marketing avenues

Tier 1 Ideas – Ideas that are most appealing to the author

Tier 2 Ideas – Ideas with strong potential, but which the author doesn't have as much enthusiasm for pursuing

Tier 3 Ideas – Ideas that were the most time-consuming, most costly, and/or which the author has the least desire to implement

There's nothing magical about this organization except that it was most appropriate for the specific product and client. The ideas could just as easily have been organized like this:

Pre-Release Ideas

Ideas to Implement in the first 30 days

Ideas to Implement days 31 through 60

etc.

If your brainstorming session was about a work situation, you might take a Tier 1, Tier 2, Tier 3 approach but modify the descriptions to relate them to ease and/or cost of implementation, how quickly the activity would generate income or increase customer satisfaction, or how many levels of approvals might be required to implement them.

Another approach to organizing the results from a corporate brainstorming session would be to organize the ideas by the departments that would implement the idea.

Organizing your list has everything to do with how implementation will happen and who will be doing it. The purpose of this step is to take your long list of ideas and organize them in such a way that you can begin to evaluate them.

In our example, we were creating a marketing plan that would be implemented by the author, so the best approach was to end our brainstorming session with a brief review of the ideas with the client, asking her to rate each idea on a scale of one to four. That enabled us to create a marketing plan that was most appropriate for her based on the ideas generated during the brainstorming session.

Evaluate and Implement

➢ Having organized the list of ideas, now it's time to pare it down to a more manageable list of only those ideas worth further evaluation. This might be accomplished by a single person (often the moderator) working alone or with a small group (some of whom may have participated in the brainstorming session). The end result of this activity should be a list of ideas that are worth your time and money to seriously evaluate.

By the way – don't throw your original list away – you never know when you might want to use some of the ideas you initially decided aren't worth pursuing.

➢ Select the five ideas that excite you the most. Then flesh out those five ideas – research how they would be implemented, what the benefits would be, what the cost would be, etc. This research will enable you to make final decisions about which ideas to implement. When you reach a blocked alley, either abandon the idea and select another or organize a smaller brainstorming session focused on unblocking the alley.

Depending on the purpose of your brainstorming, you may take the ideas back and work through them personally to select the best ones, or work with a group to choose the top ideas.

It might be appropriate to pull together a group of people with a background or personality similar to the person who generated the best idea in your initial brainstorming session. This new group of brainstormers, with similar instead of diverse backgrounds, can help "drill down" to some very creative and productive ideas within the same vein of thought.

➤ Implement the best idea or ideas. Your brainstorming has accomplished its goals by generating new and fresh ideas that have led to improvement in some area of your life or work!

Communicate with Your Brainstorming Team

➤ If your team has not been involved in the evaluation process, provide feedback to them as appropriate. This will provide satisfaction for the time they spent supporting the activity and encourage them to be involved in future brainstorming sessions.

Chapter 5
Brainstorming, Party of One

When You Don't Have a Group

If you can't find a posse to help you brainstorm, there are several techniques that spur brainstorming when working alone. The process is basically the same – your goal is to come up with as many ideas as possible. No evaluation of the ideas during your brainstorming. Set a goal for coming up with at least five totally outrageous ideas to help you get outside your own box. (Remember, though, no pressure – the purpose of the goal is simply to set yourself free from staying within the bounds of practicality. If the goal adds pressure to your individual brainstorming, don't do it!)

Since developing outrageous ideas has a way of taking us far afield if we don't have something to bring us back, start by writing out the topic about which you are going to brainstorm. This will help bring you back when you've strayed too far from your purpose. Remember, you will be playing the roles of the moderator, recorder, and the brainstormer when you're working alone. That's more than enough hats for one afternoon!

To help you view the topic from a different perspective, take four sheets of paper (or use four areas of a white board, four different windows on your computer monitor, etc.). At the top of each paper or area, write a few words that identify the perspective from which you're going to view the topic.

For example, if you are brainstorming about topics for writing a book, you might pick four perspectives from the following list:

➢ Things you know a lot about
➢ Things you have a great interest in
➢ Things you don't know much about, but would like to read or learn about
➢ The most common questions that your coworkers, managers or customers ask
➢ Topics that everyone seems to be writing about right now
➢ Topics that no one seems to be writing about right now
➢ Potential topics associated with your work life
➢ Potential topics associated with your family life
➢ Past experiences that might lend themselves to becoming a page-turner of a book

Pick any four from the list above and begin to write or type your list without regard to how good the ideas are. Within half an hour you ought to be able to come up with forty or fifty ideas!

Be sure to write down those thoughts that aren't full ideas. For example, I practiced individual brainstorming by using the above approach to brainstorming a topic for a book. I picked the first three perspectives on the list and the last one. Then I simply started coming up with ideas. One of the ideas I wrote under "things I know very little about" was "some area of technology?" No specific area of technology came to mind, but I had a sense that there were some areas I might find interesting to write about. So I wrote it down. I can go back later and look at the topic and do a second level of brainstorming on areas of technology to write about.

Review the techniques in Chapter 3 for additional ideas that might add creativity to your individual brainstorming efforts.

After about half an hour, take a break, get a cup of your favorite Starbucks blend, and check your e-mail. Then go back to your list and begin the process of selecting the five ideas that excite you the most.

Brainstorming –
Thinking Outside the Box
To Create A Different Outcome

Brainstorming can take some time, but the rewards can be tremendous. Many people thinking creatively can generate ideas that solve problems, develop fresh ideas, and create new energy.

Whether you are brainstorming in a group or alone, and whatever methods you use – enjoy it! Brainstorming is more fun than work!

Appendices Index

Appendix 1 – Checklists

Identifying Your Participants & Moderator

Moderator Responsibilities Checklist

Presentation Checklist

Brainstorming Process At-A-Glance (Moderator's Checklist)

Appendix 2 – Brainstorming Guidelines

APPENDIX 1 – Checklists

Identifying Your Participants & Moderator

☐ 3 – 6 individuals

☐ Varied backgrounds

☐ Varied experiences

☐ Varied personalities or personality types

☐ 2 – 4 people who are comfortable with one another

☐ 1 – 2 people who don't know others as well

~~~~~~~~~~~~~~

☐ Select a Moderator

Potential Participants

1. _____
2. _____
3. _____
4. _____
5. _____
6. _____
Alt 1. _____
Alt 2. _____
Alt 3. _____

Potential Moderators

1. _____
2. _____

Considerations in Selecting a Moderator

The Moderator is responsible for the following:

➢ Deciding on an approach or technique
➢ Preparing the presentation
➢ Preparing questions to spark creativity
➢ Preparing creative ideas to suggest during the session
➢ Preparing the venue
➢ Inviting group members
➢ Gathering supplies
➢ Selecting a recorder
➢ Preparing for post-brainstorming activities
➢ Presenting the topic to the group
➢ Moderating the flow of ideas during the brainstorming
➢ Closing the session well
➢ Following up with participants
➢ Initiating the idea evaluation process

Moderator Responsibilities Checklist

Prepare for the Session

☐ Decide on an approach or technique

☐ Prepare the presentation

☐ Prepare questions to help spark creativity

☐ Develop a couple of creative ideas on the topic

☐ Prepare the venue

☐ Consider ways to make the session more fun and productive

☐ Invite group members

☐ Gather supplies

☐ Select a recorder

☐ Prepare for post-brainstorming activities

☐ Select a recorder

☐ _____

☐ _____

During the Brainstorming Session

☐ Present the topic to the group

☐ Moderate the flow of ideas

☐ Spark creativity by introducing your questions or ideas

☐ Initiate evaluation of ideas if desired at this point

☐ Close the session well

☐ _____

After the Brainstorming Session

☐ Follow-up with participants

☐ Initiate the idea evaluation process

☐ _____

Presentation Checklist

- ☐ Be brief – 1 to 3 sentences.
- ☐ **Define the problem, issue or topic** – what is the purpose of the brainstorming session?

_____

_____

_____

_____

- ☐ **Restate the topic** in a slightly different way.

_____

_____

_____

_____

- ☐ **Allow time for questions** while presenting the issue.
- ☐ **Develop a question or two** to get the session started.

_____

_____

_____

_____

_____

- ☐ **Develop several questions** to foster creativity during the session.

_____

_____

_____

_____

_____

_____

- ☐ **Develop several off the wall ideas** to spark creativity.

_____

_____

_____

_____

APPENDIX 1 – *Checklists (Continued)*

Brainstorming Process At-A-Glance (Moderator's Checklist)

- ☐ Present the brainstorming topic to the group (use the *Presentation Checklist* if desired).
- ☐ Explain the guidelines for the brainstorming session (use *Brainstorming Guidelines* if desired).
- ☐ Select a recorder if you have not done so previously.
- ☐ The recorder should add every idea to the list.
- ☐ Encourage participants to shout out any and all ideas.
- ☐ Remind participants – there is no such thing as a bad (or wrong) idea in brainstorming.
- ☐ Encourage participants to express ideas that are not fully formed.
- ☐ Generally, do not allow any criticism of the ideas. If you do allow some criticism, be sure the spirit of the session remains positive.
- ☐ Generally, do not allow discussion of the ideas, except for what is required to understand it.
- ☐ Encourage participants not to be constrained by current processes, conventional wisdom, practicality, budgets or their boss's favorite approach.
- ☐ Allow time for thinking, but keep the session moving fairly quickly.
- ☐ Use your prepared questions or ideas to keep the creative flow going.
- ☐ Watch your time limit – typically, 30 – 60 minutes.
- ☐ Generally, end the brainstorming session when you've reached your time limit or exhausted your ideas, which-ever comes first.
- ☐ If appropriate, spend an additional 10 – 20 minutes organizing your list of ideas.
- ☐ End your brainstorming session by telling the group how the ideas will be evaluated and what future communication participants can expect.

Brainstorming Guidelines

The idea of brainstorming is to generate as many new, fresh and creative ideas about a topic as possible. After the moderator has presented the problem, issue or topic...

➤ The recorder will add every idea to the list.

➤ Shout out any and all ideas.

➤ There is no such thing as a bad idea in brainstorming.

➤ Don't be shy! Remember – there is no such thing as a bad idea in brainstorming.

➤ Do not to be constrained by current processes, conventional wisdom, practicality, budgets or your boss's favorite approach.

➤ Express ideas that don't seem practical.

➤ Express ideas that seem too crazy to implement.

➤ Express ideas that are counter-cultural or counter-intuitive.

➤ Express ideas that are not fully formed. Others may fill in the gaps.

➤ Generally, do not criticize ideas as they are suggested.

➤ When you find yourself tempted to criticize an idea, search for an alternative to the idea.

➤ Generally, do not discuss the ideas when they are suggested, unless it is required to understand the idea.

➤ Finding yourself overwhelmed? Sit back and block out the others for a minute or two. Think through the topic. Then pull yourself back into the group and express your ideas.

➤ If you have an idea after the session is over, communicate it to the moderator.

About
the Author

Sandra Hovatter learned project management skills as an officer in the U.S. Air Force and then as a project management consultant to the aerospace industry. She has applied these skills as a small business entrepreneur. She and her husband launched their own desktop publishing business in 1988, when the field was still in its infancy. Twenty five years later, Data Designs Publishing still serves many of the same clients they started with (along with many new ones). DDP specializes in the desktop publishing of complex long documents such as industrial parts catalogs and technical manuals, and in book publishing.

Sandra has an MA from Malone University, is an ordained minister, and blogs regularly at both her company website (www.DataDesignsPublishing.com) and her ministry website (www.ApprehendingGrace.com). In addition to being the president of Data Designs Publishing, she is a speaker and writer.

She has been married since 1978 to her wonderful husband and business partner Phil. They live in Norwalk, Ohio.